Original title:
The House at the Crossroads

Copyright © 2025 Creative Arts Management OÜ
All rights reserved.

Author: Arabella Whitmore
ISBN HARDBACK: 978-1-80587-106-4
ISBN PAPERBACK: 978-1-80587-576-5

The Doorway to Change

A door swings wide with laughter loud,
It's filled with shoes, both lost and proud.
The cat looks vexed, as squirrels race,
Through every room, they start their chase.

The fridge hums songs of days gone by,
With jars of pickles bakers cry.
A mop stands ready, on guard it seems,
In this wild place where chaos dreams.

A Tapestry of Tomorrows

Threads of fate weave funny tales,
Of mismatched socks and soggy sails.
Each stitch a giggle, every seam,
Stretched tight with snacks that burst and beam.

The clock ticks on with silly rhymes,
In empty rooms, it plays with chimes.
A tapestry bright, spun from our woes,
With candy wrappers where laughter grows.

The Celestial Compass

A compass spins, not pointing straight,
It finds the pie at the neighbor's plate.
Stars laugh above, a cosmic jest,
While lost socks plot their little quest.

The moon shines down on goofy dreams,
Where every shadow dances and beams.
Directions given by wobbly sage,
Keep all wanderers in high-flying rage.

Nestled Between Choices

Two paths meet at a puppy's bark,
One leads to joy, the other, a lark.
Debates ensue over cookie bliss,
Which road to take? They ponder this.

Trapped in between a hard decision,
They flip a coin with such precision.
Heads or tails, they'll take a chance,
To end up lost in silly dance.

The Merging Lanes

Two roads collide with a honk and a wave,
Where directions get mixed and no one can save.
A chicken in a beret leads the parade,
As squirrels hold a meeting, plans seem delayed.

Traffic signs spin like a carnival ride,
While lost in a map, folks giggle and chide.
One car cries, 'I need caffeine, quick!'
Then zooms off in frenzy, a playful trick!

Navigating by Starlight

Stars are the guides in the zany night,
With constellations that argue with fright.
A cat in a cape and a dog with a hat,
Plot their escape from the pesky old rat.

Mice shout directions, but they're totally wrong,
While bats play the chorus of a peculiar song.
Under this moon, they spin tales quite absurd,
As laughter erupts with each quirky word.

Whispers of the Unseen

Echoes of giggles creep through the walls,
A ghost in a tutu performs at the halls.
With marshmallow voices, they tell cheeky lies,
As pumpkins roll by, wearing silly disguises.

Unseen merriment dances through the night,
As shadows swap stories, not one is polite.
They swap old ghost tales with a wink and a grin,
Chasing away dread, let the laughter begin!

Footsteps in the Haze

In the fog, there are footsteps that prance,
Each turn a surprise, a mysterious dance.
A jellybean bard sings under a tree,
While frogs in top hats debate what's to eat.

The mist holds the secrets of tickles and fun,
As one bumbles forward, a quick little run.
Beneath a slapstick moon, all senses align,
In this wacky wonder, everything's fine!

The Diverging Stream

Two paths ahead, what shall I choose?
One leads to joy, the other, some blues.
A squirrel giggles, points with a paw,
As I trip on a branch, and fall with a flaw.

In the garden of choices, weeds grow tall,
I'm lost in a maze, or is it a ball?
Each turn brings a grin, a chuckle or two,
Sometimes it's messy, yet often feels new.

Songs of Serendipity

A tune in my heart, a skip in my step,
I dance through the chaos, no need for a prep.
A bird sings off-key, but I hum along,
In this silly ballet, I feel I belong.

With every wrong turn, a rhyme does appear,
A neighbor's bad karaoke brings laughter, oh dear!
We twirl and we spin, on this merry-go-round,
In the wackiest circus, pure joy can be found.

Echoes from the Past

In dusty old corners, ghosts take a peek,
They chuckle at mishaps when we try to speak.
A wig falls off Grandpa, right onto the cat,
As memories echo, 'Was that really that?'

With laughter we gather, around tales of yore,
Each year brings a story, who knew there were more?
These echoes of giggles, reminders so bright,
Of how we were silly, in the soft, fading light.

The Turning Point

At the fork in the road, a chicken struts by,
With a wink and a cluck, it's hard not to sigh.
Do I dare to follow? What's next on this quest?
Perhaps I'll end up just winging the rest.

Twists and turns lead me, like a dance on a stage,
Each step brings a laugh, each choice a new page.
So here's to the quirks, the twists we embrace,
In this wobbly journey, we all find our place.

Shadows of Unchosen Roads

Two paths diverged, a squirrel on a spree,
Knocking over acorns, oh what a sight to see!
One way leads to cookies, the other to beans,
Decisions, decisions, with funny routines!

A cat with a map, full of purrs and sass,
Waving goodbye to the lovers who pass.
'Choose wisely,' it laughs, 'there's wisdom in fun,
No way's a wrong way—just run, run, run!'

The Doorway of Possibilities

A door swings wide, it creaks and it groans,
Behind it are cupcakes and funny old clones.
One in a tutu, another with a hat,
Singing out loud, quite the crazy spat!

You step inside, and what do you see?
A fish playing poker, stole the last eclair, whee!
With laughter that echoes all over the space,
The gateways of laughter, a comical race.

Whispers of the Forking Trail

A sign ahead reads, 'Right for pie, left for cheese!'
A goat in a jacket snorts, brings you to your knees.
On the right, there's laughter, on the left, just moans,
As ants throw confetti on mushroom-filled thrones!

With each little step, the decisions delight,
'Where's the party?' you ask in the night.
Frogs leap for joy as you wiggle and sway,
Whispers of joy lead you further away!

A Place of Paradox

A junction where kisses meet with high fives,
Where cupcakes fly and spaghetti dives.
A jester juggles while penguins compete,
In a land full of giggles, oh what a feat!

Logic takes a nap as chaos takes wing,
Balloons filled with laughter start dancing and sing.
Who knew the crossroads could pull such a prank?
In this wild muddle, we all share a tank!

Bridge Between Worlds

At dusk, a bridge swings wide,
Where silly geese do glide.
They speak of dreams and sun,
With laughter spun just for fun.

A man with socks that clash,
Tells tales of a squirrel's stash.
He juggles eggs with flair,
The crowd can't help but stare.

Cats and dogs in a race,
Chasing shadows, a wild chase.
They leap across the seam,
In a whimsical daydream.

With each step taken bright,
The worlds collide in delight.
A groove that makes you sway,
In this funny, sunny play.

The Timekeeper's Realm

In a realm where time hops,
The clocks spin and do flops.
A rabbit wears a tie,
While dancing with a pie.

Time flies on roller skates,
While turtles chew on fates.
They argue who is slow,
In this absurd show.

Spoons tick-tock on the wall,
As teapots start to brawl.
With laughter, they conspire,
In a dance of pure satire.

Each tick brings a new jest,
As seconds play a quest.
In a quirky parade,
Time's a joke masquerade.

Spirals of Intent

In a spiral, thoughts do twirl,
Like dancing leaves that whirl.
Intentions flip and flop,
In a playful, tricky crop.

Pigs in tutus leap and sway,
Conducting clouds of hay.
They tip their hats to dreams,
While rolling down in beams.

A clown attempts to bake,
But muffins start to quake.
They giggle, puff, and pop,
In this upside-down shop.

Spirals lead to laughter's door,
Where silly reins abound galore.
Let's twirl and spin around,
In joy that's lost and found.

Canvas of Connections

On a canvas bright and bold,
Splatters of dreams unfold.
Cacti wear bright hats,
While dancing with the cats.

Colors clash in dainty fights,
As owls debate the nights.
Each stroke a giggle's spark,
In this whimsical park.

A painter with wobbly shoes,
Mixes greens with purple hues.
With each twist and turn,
Laughter's flame will burn.

Connections burst in cheer,
As friends draw near, oh dear!
In this tapestry of fun,
All colors under the sun.

Signposts of Memory

Lost socks on the floor, a sight to behold,
A map of our life, both funny and bold.
The cat thinks it's hers, that chair in the hall,
She stares with a regal, judgmental call.

A pancake on the ceiling, a breakfast gone wild,
With syrupy tales of the chaos we've styled.
The doorbell rings loud, it's the dog on a spree,
Chasing shadows of squirrels, as happy as can be.

There's a mirror that giggles when it sees my hair,
Reflecting old stories, of laughter and care.
While dust bunnies dance, they twirl to the tune,
Of a life full of mishaps, under the moon.

So let's toast to this space, where mishaps unite,
In the chaos of moments, we find pure delight.
With mismatched old furniture, a quilt and a grin,
In this quirky abode, our joy will begin.

The Intersection of Dreams

Here intersect dreams with a wobble and spin,
Where the cat in a hat always wears a grin.
A lost pair of glasses, where could they have gone?
They peek from a teacup, 'What's taking you long?'

Juggling chores like a circus, oh what a sight,
I trip on a broomstick, laugh loud at my plight.
The toaster is singing a tune from the past,
While the coffee pot simmers, that aroma cast.

With piggy bank pirates and treasures galore,
We open the closet to a soft, creaky door.
Inside, every sweater has its own little tale,
Of adventures and journeys, like a vibrant gale.

As the clock strikes a rhythm on a wall so gray,
Let's dance with the echoes that waltz through the day.
In this whimsical realm, each moment's a gem,
At the gateway of dreams, we just laugh and condemn.

Where Roads Collide

Two paths diverged, in a kitchen confined,
One leads to the pantry, the other behind.
I chose the fridge route, it's chilly and bright,
Where leftovers linger and dance in the night.

The blender's a boaster, it whirs with delight,
While socks find adventure in a hilarious fight.
The spatula's plotting a coup on the rack,
While the bread rolls are giggling, 'Who's got our back?'

The dining room table's a stable of tales,
Of feasts gone awry and ketchup travails.
With forks as my audience, I take my grand bow,
As the chandelier twinkles, 'What a show, wow!'

In this quirky crossroads, life juggles its clout,
With laughter as currency, there's never a drought.
So raise up a toast with a glass of cold cheer,
In this playful confusion, we hold our dreams dear.

Reflections in the Entryway

In the entryway mirror, my hair stands on end,
A salute to my style, oh how it pretends!
My shoes cling to the mat, a complaint on repeat,
'Why do we tour the house? We just want our seat!'

The umbrella's forgotten, a tale of the rain,
While coats have a party—oh, what a campaign!
With hats stacked like stories, they whisper and boast,
About snowy adventures and the warmth of the host.

As keys play hide-and-seek in a bowl full of cheer,
I trip on the welcome mat, 'Oh no, not here!'
But laughter erupts, like a song in the air,
In the entryway chaos, we tango with flair.

So here in this space, where all journeys commence,
We find friendship and folly, a world so intense.
With joy as our compass and smiles on display,
In the realm of reflections, we'll frolic and play.

Crossroads of Dreams

In a slice of afternoon light,
A cat in a hat took flight.
He danced on a fence, oh what a sight,
Chasing shadows from morning to night.

A chicken in shoes made a fuss,
Said, 'I can't drive, but I can discuss!'
With a wave and a honk, off he rushed,
Leaving behind a puzzled hush.

At the fork with a sign that blinks,
A jester juggles while everyone thinks.
'Clear your minds, let go of the kinks,
Choose a path that never sinks!'

As laughter echoes down the lane,
A dog with a wig joins in the game.
At the crossroads, nothing's the same,
Each turn's a twist in the silly fame.

Threshold of Fate

At the door where choices pile,
A shoe salesman greets with a smile.
'Pick a pair, stay for a while,
Let's stroll down dreams with style!'

A hedgehog named Fred, so bold and spry,
Wore a bowtie and had a tie-dye.
'Fate's just a dare, so give it a try,
I've got the route, just you comply!'

With giggles and wiggles, the choice began,
A tap dance on grass by a flirting fan.
Life's a romp, not a detailed plan,
Let your feet lead—yes, that's the jam!

When the clock strikes one, hear the chime,
Even ghosts join the silly rhyme.
Destinies here are silly, sublime,
Just grab your shoes—it's party time!

Where Paths Converge

In a wigwam of stories spun tight,
A squirrel wore specs, oh, what a sight!
He read maps upside down in delight,
While telling the tale of a bird taking flight.

Two owls discussed whether it's fate,
Or just a big joke served up on a plate.
'Choose whichever, just don't be late,
We've got snacks for whatever we create!'

Around the bend, a llama sings,
In sequined shoes that jingle like rings.
'Whether it's paths or wild flapping wings,
Join me and see what a good laugh brings!'

So paths join hands, a quirky parade,
Under the sun where friendships are made.
Each step a giggle, no need to be weighed,
At this whimsical junction of joys that won't fade.

Echoes in the Hallway

In a house where echoes play fun tricks,
A mop with a hat pulls neat little kicks.
Spinning tales of hide-and-seek flicks,
It sweeps up laughter like a bag of tricks.

A pair of socks began to argue,
One was polka-dots, the other bright blue.
'Choose the color that fits your view,
At this crossroad, there's much to pursue!'

Meanwhile, a raccoon with a wink and a grin,
Set up a shop, let the humor begin.
'Stories and snacks! Come take a spin,
Life's but a circus where all can win!'

So echoes bounce back, a playful delight,
In hallways where silliness takes flight.
Join the mirth as shadows ignite,
At this crossroads, everything feels right!

A Space Between Dreams

In a place where two paths collide,
One leads to bread, the other, a slide.
You'd think they would settle, have tea,
But they argue which way is more free.

One says 'Go right, the grass is a treat!'
The other insists, 'No, left has more sweet!'
While squirrels debate with acorn in hand,
The moon chuckles down, it's quite unplanned.

A cat leans on signposts, conning a mouse,
At midnight, they're dancing, a waltz through the house.
While shadows are laughing, they tease and they twirl,
In a space where dreams meet, watch chaos unfurl.

So if you find yourself caught in a spat,
Just take a deep breath and don't lose your hat!
For in the madness of laughter's embrace,
You might just discover your own silly place.

Roots of Revelation

In the ground where the wisdom grows,
Laughter and giggles sprout from the toes.
Each root whispers secrets, some silly, some grand,
Like how to find joy with a non-performing band.

The trees provide shade for thoughts that roam wide,
While critters debate whose nest is the pride.
With nuts of great fortune, the gathered will feast,
On stories of nature, the laughable beast.

Two flowers argue which color is best,
While a worm claims he's down for the jest.
In this mix-up of petals and pride,
Even the thorns want to join in the ride.

So if you ever get lost on your way,
Join the roots and the worms for a quirky ballet.
For in this wild garden where humor runs free,
The truth is just nonsense, so come dance with me!

The Junction's Embrace

At the corner where mismatched socks meet,
A pigeon on a mission, oh what a treat!
A cat in a bow tie dances with flair,
While traffic lights giggle, causing some scare.

A busker plays tunes with a quirky beat,
While squirrels in sunglasses prepare for a feat.
Lost tourists whirl round, searching for signs,
As laughter erupts from the pizza behind.

Raccoons in top hats sneak by for a snack,
Balancing donuts, they're leading the pack.
The postman's too busy jesting with glee,
As he juggles the letters like a circus marquee.

Doors of Destiny

There's a door that squeaks with tales to tell,
Each knob spins tales from its haphazard hell.
One opens to a dance of furrowed brows,
the other shows fish in colorful cows.

A door with a parrot offers wisecracks loud,
While another dispenses tacos to the crowd.
In this charming bazaar, you'd trade with delight,
For a giggle or two from the ghost in the night.

Behind one, a clown makes balloon animals,
While in another, a chef burns the manuals.
Not quite what you'd expect, a surprise each time,
Walking through those doors feels just like a rhyme.

Shadows of Dilemma

A shadow dances, twirling with flair,
It wears mismatched shoes—a wayward affair.
One foot in the bakery, the other in gloom,
Deciding which path would lead to their doom.

A pickle debates between sweet and sour,
In the corner, a cactus claims victory, feels power.
Should it jump for the fridge or lounge by the sink?
While raccoons hold court, just to argue and think.

A hedgehog debates with a very wise chair,
While the shadows are laughing; oh, what a snare!
In the dim of the night, there's chaos and fun,
As dilemmas dissolve, and all shadows run.

Between the Lines of Fate

In a book where the plot seems to jiggle and sway,
A penguin in goggles leads the fray.
Pages flip, and giggles burst forth with delight,
As chapters unfold under disco ball light.

Characters bicker over cake and pie,
While a grumpy old whale swims high in the sky.
Fate's an odd river with sprinkles and limes,
That sloshes and giggles, confusing all rhymes.

Amidst the tomfoolery, tales twist and turn,
Where fortunes are mixed like a chaotic churn.
Between the lines, oh, the laughter abounds,
In this world of whimsy, where joy knows no bounds.

The Crossroads of Solitude

In a mix of socks and shoes,
All directions seem to lose.
You can turn left or right,
But which way leads to light?

A chicken crossed with a grin,
Wondering where to begin.
No GPS can help you here,
Just a map shaped like a deer!

The cat meows with great support,
As I seek a road to sort.
Maybe I'll just call a cab,
And forget this silly drab!

So I laugh and spin around,
In this jigsaw puzzle found.
Getting lost is quite the game,
In this world where all's the same!

Murmurs in the Maze

In a twisty maze I dwell,
Hearing whispers, can you tell?
A ghost says, 'Try a left!'
Another claims, 'You're quite bereft!'

Pigeons squawk a concert plan,
While I dance like a crazy man.
The corners twist; my patience wanes,
Yet laughter bubbles through my veins!

I bump into a hedge of cheese,
And shout, 'Oh, what a tasty tease!'
Rats in hats begin to jest,
In this furry, funny fest!

With giggles echoing around,
Each uproarious sight I found.
In this maze, I choose the glee,
For laughter is the best decree!

The Lattice of Fate

A web of choices all around,
Each decision makes a sound.
Should I leap or take a stroll?
Maybe tangle with a mole!

The weaver's spinning foolishly,
Telling jokes, oh so dizzy.
Every thread a tale untold,
With a punchline made of gold!

Shall I follow the squirrel's lead,
Or listen to the daisies plead?
With fates entwined like ribbons bright,
I laugh at wrongs turned to right!

So here I bounce through every strand,
With a chuckle, life is planned.
In this lattice, joy's my fate,
And that's just simply great!

Colliding Currents

Two rivers meet, oh what a scene,
Splashing fish that dance and scream.
One is calm, the other wild,
Together, they're a playful child!

The currents clash with joyful yells,
Tickling waters; everyone swells.
Frogs in hats, they croak along,
As whirlpools twist to a silly song!

A boat full of jellies floats by,
With jellybeans to fill the sky.
Bubbles pop and laughter spills,
In these waters, joy fulfills!

So let the streams all intertwine,
Creating chaos that is fine.
In colliding currents, cheer's our tune,
A splashy dance beneath the moon!

Lanterns of Potential

Beneath the glowing lanterns bright,
I ponder my choices, day and night.
Which path to take? Oh, what a jest!
Should I eat the cake or skip the quest?

A squirrel stole my sandwich! How rude!
He danced on my plans, oh what a mood!
With each twist and turn, I laugh and grin,
Life's silly dance, let the chaos begin!

The compass spins like a roller skate,
Points to the pizza, isn't that fate?
With options galore, it's hard to steer,
But who needs direction when snacks are near?

With lanterns lit, I'll just sashay,
Embracing the weirdness day by day.
Let the night unfold, adventure's begun,
In this whimsical life, I'm having fun!

Whispers of Choices

In a land where whispers float like kites,
Decisions chuckle beneath twinkling lights.
Should I wear socks with sandals today?
Or opt for style in a daring way?

A cactus waved hello, poked my arm,
While frogs debate charm with a croaky charm.
Each murmur a riddle in the playful breeze,
Swapping my sanity for some giggly peas.

Should I leap to the left or skip to the right?
A dance with my shadow in the moonlight.
With chortles echoing from the trees so wide,
I can't help but laugh at this whimsical ride!

Whispers of choices, each turn a delight,
Guiding my steps through the silliness bright.
With chuckles and grins, I forge my own way,
In this chaos of fun, let's dance and play!

Echoes in the Threshold

At the threshold where echoes play,
I trip on my thoughts and sway all day.
Each decision rings like a bell, a chime,
Who knew that missing socks could be so prime?

With echoes of laughter bouncing around,
A parade of choices led by a clown.
Should I wear polka dots or stripes today?
Oh what a conundrum, come what may!

The doorknob spins, it's got some flair,
It whispers, "Choose wisely! Or maybe not care!"
I'll follow the giggles, they know the score,
With echoes guiding, who needs a door?

As I stand at the edge of this quirky spree,
With a wink from the universe, I think I'll be free.
Let the echoes ring out, bringing joy anew,
In this maze of giggles, I'll find my due.

Pathways Converge

In the lanes where the pathways meet,
I stumbled on humor in the heartbeat.
Two roads diverged and they just giggled,
Offered me cookies, my taste buds wiggled!

One path leads to a jungle of bees,
The other to doughnuts, oh, what a tease!
Choices like candy, so shiny and bright,
With sprinkles of laughter, they dance in the night.

I twirl down the route where the donuts call,
Wondering how I might trip or fall.
But life's about laughs, some tumbles are fun,
Each giggle a step, shining like the sun!

Pathways converge in this merry domain,
With flavors of joy that will never wane.
I'll skip and I'll hop where the chuckles arise,
In the banquet of choices, laughter's the prize!

Portraits of the Unchosen

In corners, dustbunnies dance with glee,
Unwanted socks share tales of a spree.
Tangled in laundry, they plot and conspire,
While mismatched shoes rest by the fire.

A cat in a hat critiques the scene,
Pondering choices that might have been keen.
As crumbs serenade the floor's vast expanse,
Who knew rejection could lead to a dance?

Forgotten plants try hard to survive,
Potting soil dreams of being alive.
Wilting romances with sunlight denied,
Why must alternatives always be tried?

Knickknacks gossip about what's a hit,
A vase full of marbles claims it's quite fit.
Colorful choices lay strewn all around,
Yet laughter erupts in the mess that we've found.

Cradled in Uncertainty

A squirrel on the fence weighs his next leap,
Contemplating acorns, a secret he keeps.
At breakfast, my toast refuses to pop,
Just like my ambitions that somehow just flop.

In dreams, I ride camels that barely can trot,
While elephants dance in a rather fine plot.
Each morning, I wonder what fate has in mind,
Whether chaos or calm will be the day's bind.

A sock on the ceiling? A mystery's touch!
The meaning of life? I can't think too much.
With crayons I scrawl my uncertain design,
Embracing the whims that all twist and entwine.

Yet laughter echoes through every mishap,
My plans, like my pancakes, all fall into flap.
Cradled by chaos, I find it's just fine,
When doubt takes a seat, and the giggles align.

The Map of Our Making

With paper and crayon, we sketch out a quest,
Imaginary lands where we fancy our best.
Yet paths made of spaghetti twist round to the fridge,
For adventures in snacking, we leap like a bridge.

X marks the spot where the dog lost a bone,
While cats plot their routes with a highly sharp tone.
Puddles become oceans of make-believe tides,
As children set sail on their bicycles' rides.

We navigate bedtimes with stories galore,
Each chapter unraveled brings laughter and more.
Maps scribbled in joy show no paths but swirls,
Through forests of toys and sparkly pearls.

So let's chart our course with a grin and a laugh,
For the best of our journey may just be the path.
In the atlas of living, odd routes often shine,
With my quirky companions, this life is divine.

The Balancing Act of Life

On a tightrope made of stretched-out string cheese,
Juggling my breakfast while hoping for ease.
Coffee cups teeter as laughter takes flight,
Who knew that today would be such a delight?

With socks on my hands and shoes on my head,
I ponder the wisdom my pet fish once said.
"To waltz through the day is a skill, don't you see?
Just dance like nobody's giving you degree!"

Balancing crumbs while chasing the cat,
Confetti of chaos: imagine that!
A leap over laundry becomes quite the feat,
As I duck from the dog with shoes on my feet.

And when the day's done, I'll chuckle out loud,
Life's circus is glorious, chaotic, and proud.
So I'll tiptoe through it, with a grin ear to ear,
For each funny moment's a gift wrapped in cheer.

Twilight at the T-junction

Under the glow of a flickering sign,
A chicken crossed, looking quite fine.
She paused in the middle, struck a pose,
As if to declare, 'Nowhere to go, who knows?'

Traffic stopped, a curious scene,
Drivers laughing, it felt like a dream.
A duck joined in, quacking with glee,
In this wacky ballet, we found unity!

A squirrel skated on a skateboard's rim,
And someone shouted, 'Hey, you be him!'
With each honk of horns, the world felt right,
In this silly pause, as day turned to night.

So here's to the junction, the laughter we share,
Where chickens and ducks dance without a care.
With twilight settling, the fun's just begun,
At this crazy crossroads, we've all found our fun!

The Lantern's Light

In a glow of yellow, bright and round,
A lantern swung, making silly sounds.
It lit up a cat with its tail held high,
As if she were saying, 'See me fly by!'

A raccoon peeked in, eyes wide with delight,
Thinking the lantern looked good for a bite.
It reached for the bulb, but in horror we saw,
The cat leapt and swatted, 'Not on my paw!'

Reflection shimmered, dreams took flight,
As all of us gathered to share in the light.
With giggles erupting, we danced in a spree,
While the lantern just chuckled, 'You all belong to me!'

So here's to the glow, and antics so bright,
Where every strange shadow brings us delight.
In this radiant glow, let's choose to be brave,
For laughter's the treasure that we all crave!

Encounters at the Exit

At the bend where laughter meets the way,
A frog in a tux said, 'Come join my ballet!'
With leaps and bounds, he danced on the grass,
While nearby a snail took his time, letting it pass.

Cars lined up, their drivers confused,
As a hedgehog spun tales, highly enthused.
'I told you this route is the way to success!'
But the way that he danced, left us all in distress.

A bird flew down, with a map in her beak,
'Follow me, friends, to where trouble's meek!'
But we just seemed stuck, in this exit parade,
Where giggles erupted, and seriousness swayed.

So cheers to these moments, so quirky and wild,
Where animals gather, both silly and styled.
At this exit sign, let joy be the guide,
And we'll ride this fun wave, with laughter as our stride!

Pathways and Portals

On pathways winding beneath a bright sun,
We stumbled upon a party, oh what fun!
With fairies and gnomes dancing in line,
And a worm in a hat, sipping on brine.

'Who invited the snail?' asked a doe with a grin,
As he spun to the music, his shell a bright win.
'He brings the good vibes, and the snacks from his pack,'
In this hilarious gathering, no one looked back.

A portal appeared, swirling and wide,
'Jump in, my friends, let's take a fun ride!'
So off we all went, on this wild escapade,
Through laughter-lined lanes, where good times were made.

So here's to the paths, the portals we find,
Where giggles and joy grow in every kind.
With whims as our guide, in this creature-filled town,
Let's revel in laughter, let joy know no bounds!

Moments on the Threshold

A door swings wide, what luck it seems,
With socks on feet, I trip on dreams.
My cat gives chase, my tea's gone cold,
One step inside, the tales unfold.

A neighbor shouts, his hair a fright,
"Did you see that ghost in the moonlight?"
I laugh and nod, what a silly fable,
As he runs off, like a kid in a stable.

Do dishes dance when no one is near?
I might just ask, or it's all in my ear.
A sandwich winks, the clock strikes four,
Stuck in this riddle, forever to explore.

With laughter echoing through every crack,
This quirky space, I never look back.
In the chaos, there lies such peace,
Embracing the odd, my worries cease.

Connections in the Void

At the corner where all met and parted,
A rubber chicken left, highly charted.
The street lamp flickers like an old sitcom,
While pigeons plot, oh the wise little con!

They tell me jokes about clouds and cheese,
While I'm stuck here, with the buzzing bees.
My thoughts disconnect, then reconnect fast,
Like Wi-Fi signals, always a blast.

Who's behind the curtain, tugging my strings?
A dog in a bowtie, that's the real thing!
With a wag and a bark, he steals the show,
In the void of night, where silliness flows.

Yet amidst this strange, cosmic plight,
I wonder if aliens laugh at our flight.
We gallop through space, in mismatched shoes,
In a web of quirks, it's the best kind of blues.

Portraits of a Dilemma

Two paths diverge, like socks askew,
One leads to pie, the other to stew.
A giant fork in this road's design,
Who knew a choice could taste so divine?

A bird with a hat, perched on a sign,
Sings sweetly about a life so fine.
"Take the left road, where the cake is king!"
I tilt my head, it's a confused fling.

Sketchbooks filled with my wildest thoughts,
A scribble of chaos, but never distraught.
Do I embrace the sandwiches rare?
Or dance with the fish in a fountain affair?

In indecision, the laughs blend anew,
As food makes a home, with a friend or two.
The portraits I paint, a silly delight,
In the mixing of flavors, I find my light.

The Meeting of Two Realities

A couch in the sky, a rug on the floor,
The cat wears sunglasses, ready for more.
I've brewed tea with stars, or maybe it's dreams,
Reality bends with its quirky themes.

A dance on a cloud, to a polka beat,
Where squirrels are hosts with two left feet.
We laugh at the chaos, twirling around,
In this meeting, we're blissfully bound.

The sun throws confetti, the moon wears a skirt,
I trip over laughter, get lost in the dirt.
What's real and what's not? A grand cosmic jest,
In this muddled mash, I'm feeling blessed.

As worlds collide with a bang and a boom,
I dance with the cats in my colorful room.
Together we twirl, in absurdity's glow,
In this funny realm, we endlessly flow.

The Meeting of Winds

Two breezes met with a spin,
One wore a hat, the other a grin.
They twirled and danced, causing confusion,
Swapping tales of their windy delusion.

A gust from the east joined the fun,
Blew hats off heads, oh what a run!
With laughter and whoops, they took to the skies,
While passing birds blinked in surprise.

Clouds rolled in, joining the play,
A circus of chaos on that day.
In circles they whirled, creating a show,
Where laughter echoed, and troubles let go.

Finally, they gusted their way out of sight,
Leaving behind a delightful delight.
As quiet fell, all simply sighed,
For the winds had left with a tickle and glide.

Unraveled Decisions

A signpost stood, all crooked and bent,
A squirrel stood there, looking quite spent.
One way to nuts, the other to snacks,
Decisions made with whimsical quacks.

Two paths diverged, one muddy, one clear,
The squirrel scratched his head, full of fear.
He flipped a coin and it flew like a jet,
Came down in a puddle—oh what a wet!

He screamed and squeaked at his fate so grim,
What led him here? Was it the whim?
With a leap and a bound, he scattered away,
Leaving the signs in disarray.

And as he dashed, the world laughed aloud,
At the little beast lost, but ever so proud.
For sometimes the journey's the best part of all,
Even if you end up with a nutty squall.

Stories Woven in Walls

The walls could chatter with tales galore,
Of sock puppets plotting and fish that soar.
Each crack a whisper, each stain a phase,
Telling stories of mischief and hilarious ways.

A door creaked open, old hinges groaned,
Out popped a cat that had overthrown.
"Whiskers and giggles," it smirked with pride,
"I've seen things that make me want to hide!"

There was laughter of beans stored up on a shelf,
Who recently learned to laugh at themselves.
With winks and nods, their fun took flight,
As walls echoed giggles, deep into the night.

Each room a chapter, each nook a jest,
In this realm of walls, the silly felt blessed.
Not just bricks and mortar, but stories untold,
Where merriment lives, and adventures unfold.

The Fork in the Road

At the fork, two paths caught my eye,
One smelled of pie, the other of rye.
One side was sunny, the other a gloom,
I pondered my steps, predicting my doom.

A turtle ambled with a smirk on his face,
Said, "Take the pie route, it's a sweet embrace!"
But a rabbit zipping by shouted, "No, no!
The rye will give you a splendid show!"

With each passing critter, my mind was a stew,
So many choices, what was I to do?
I grabbed at my hat, flipped it in the air,
And leaped down the center, without a care!

Now here I stand, in a comical mess,
With breadcrumbs and laughter, I must confess.
For sometimes the best place isn't set,
But the joy in the journey, that's where you're met.

Secrets Beneath the Eaves

Under the roof, the whispers fly,
A squirrel's gossip, oh my, oh my!
The cat joins in with a meow and a purr,
While the dog just snores, not a care, not a blur.

Mice make a plan for a daring heist,
To nibble the cheese before it gets sliced!
The chandelier sways, a lighthearted tease,
As laughter echoes through the rigging of trees.

Old boots hang crooked; they're tired and worn,
But they gossip of journeys, adventure reborn.
And when rain patters, the roof starts to laugh,
The secrets it keeps are quite the quaff!

So gather your friends, let stories unfold,
Beneath all the eaves, there's mischief untold.
In the comical chaos of life's wild parade,
Lies the essence of joy, unafraid and unfrayed.

A Tale of Two Directions

Two paths diverged on a windy lane,
One led to cookies, the other to grain.
A chicken in sneakers crossed just for fun,
While a goat on a scooter was racing the sun.

To the left, there's laughter, a carnival scene,
To the right, a nap by a tree, nice and green.
A sheep in a top hat declares with a grin,
'This is a riddle! Come join in the spin!'

The signs are silly, all painted in jest,
"Frog jumps this way, the snail takes a rest."
With each silly step, choices dance on the ground,
In this weird world where friends abound.

So follow your nose, or what tickles your toes,
The journey's a giggle, wherever it goes.
With joy in the air and laughter galore,
Choose wisely, dear traveler, there's fun to explore.

The Confluence of Heartbeats

In a room full of friends, the heartbeats collide,
A symphony plays, laughter fills up the tide.
Tacos and jokes swirl around in a dance,
Making mischief is their quirky romance.

One says, "I tripped, and the cat stole my shoe!"
Another just winks, "Well, the dog's missing too!"
A chorus erupts, full of giggles and sighs,
As the fish in the tank communicate lies.

With every heartbeat, a new story brews,
Conflict and resolution, in colorful hues.
The blender is whirring, smoothies in sight,
Blending the chaos till everything's right.

As tales intertwine, the magic's in play,
A tapestry woven from laughter today.
With friends by your side, heartbeats align,
In this joyful chaos, everything's fine.

Facades of Choices

Behind each choice lies a funny disguise,
With wigs and mustaches, tricking our eyes.
A turtle in shades thinks he's found the best road,
While a rabbit in socks carries all of the load.

The signs say, "Turn back!" but who's to obey?
A hedgehog in slippers insists it's the way.
With a wink and a nod, decisions unfold,
In a circus of paths where both brave and bold.

One door leads to flowers, the other to cheese,
As the taste of adventure fills every breeze.
The choices we make can be grand or absurd,
Each one a tale, waiting to be heard.

So giggle with glee at the decisions we face,
Life's a collage, a whimsical place.
With laughter as compass, we wander and roam,
Embrace every choice, for we're never alone.

The Hearth's Silent Counsel

In a room where shadows dance,
Chairs whisper secrets, take a chance.
The cat sits high, a royal queen,
Laughing softly, a hidden scene.

A teapot sings, its spout ajar,
While dogs bark loud, a silly car.
Footprints track in and out of sight,
As dinner burns, oh what a plight!

The couch is wise, it creaks with age,
Every cushion tells a tale or page.
Flip-flops tumble, a hallway race,
The floor's a stage, a funny place.

Yet as night falls, laughter stays,
In silent counsel, everyone plays.
Pillow fights bloom, hearts align,
In the chaos, all is fine.

Guiding Stars Above

A lightbulb flickers, a star in plight,
It mimics planets, oh what a sight!
The remote control, lost in the fray,
Navigates dreams, guiding the way.

Outside the window, moonbeams chatter,
While raccoons plot, in their quiet clatter.
Planets align for a late-night feast,
As neighbors argue with their pet beast.

Telescope's ready, it aims for the skies,
But sees only socks—oh what a surprise!
Constellations laugh, twinkling bright,
While Jupiter's just a round light.

"Starship" is just mom's old car,
With '90s CDs, it won't go far.
Yet in this chaos, dreams take flight,
Under guiding stars, everything feels right.

The Threshold of Tomorrow

At the door, life tiptoes near,
Whispers of tomorrow fill the sphere.
The doormat laughs at muddy shoes,
While keys jingle, sharing news.

A postman waves, he's in on the plan,
Delivering letters from a tough old man.
Life's karaoke, a wild duet,
With hiccups and giggles, no regret.

The horizon stretches, wide and bright,
Filled with promise, cast in light.
Yet every step, a silly dance,
Where socks don't match; it's pure romance.

A cat darts past, chasing the sun,
Its leap and bound, a joyous run.
Every moment a playful sway,
In the threshold of a brand new day.

Uncharted Destinies

With maps upside down, we roam the hall,
Exploring the fridge, we heed the call.
Leftover pizza, a treasure to find,
As tummies grumble, we unwind.

Board games scattered, pieces askew,
As laughter echoes, we start anew.
The dice roll wild, chance takes the lead,
Bumps and falls, oh what a breed!

In gardens wild, dreams take root,
A frog wears a crown—how cute!
While gnomes converse in secret schemes,
Underneath the moonlight beams.

With each misstep, we forge a way,
In uncharted lands, come what may.
For in this mess, we truly thrive,
Adventures shared, we feel alive.

A Gathering of Tides

When the seagulls squawk, what a sight,
They argue and dance in the fading light.
Waves crash and tumble, making a fuss,
Surfers all giggle, not one has a bus.

In the sand, there's a crab with a hat,
He struts like a king, how about that?
With a flip-flop throne, he rules the shore,
While tourists all stare, heartily roar.

Seashells are treasures, or so they claim,
Watch as they fight to make a name.
'I'm a dollar!' one shouts, 'Just look at my shine!'
Sandy and silly, it's a grand, wild line.

As night sinks in, and laughter takes flight,
A bonfire's glow ignites their delight.
With marshmallows roasted, and stories so sly,
The beach will remember, as waves ebb and sigh.

The Mirage of What-Could-Be

In a meadow where daisies have dreams,
Lies a squirrel who plots, or so it seems.
He peers through his glasses, with nuts stacked high,
'Tomorrow I'll build a jetpack to fly!'

A rabbit jumps by, the plan is absurd,
With whiskers twitching, she says not a word.
While turtles sit slow, in their shell-shaded shade,
And giggle, 'Good luck with your airborne crusade!'

The sun winks down, and the flowers all sway,
While the sky whispers softly, 'Maybe today?'
With visions of rocket-fueled hops in their heads,
They chase after dreams, instead of their beds.

But time ticks away, and the sun starts to yawn,
Our squirrel still hopeful, for each bright dawn.
'Next week for sure, I'm convinced I will soar!'
While friends just roll eyes, 'We've heard it before!'

The Lantern's Dilemma

A lantern once shone in a rickety shed,
With visions of light, but it feared being dead.
'Inferno or dim, which path shall I take?
If I flicker too much, will they all start to quake?'

A moth buzzed around with teasing delight,
'Turn up the juice, let's dance in the night!
With shadows to dodge and sparks to fly,
Join us, dear buddy, don't be shy!'

The old dusty cobwebs just sighed in despair,
As spiders all giggled, spun stories in air.
'You light up the room, when you're not so shy,
Just don't burn your wick, or you'll say bye-bye!'

Yet cracks in the glass revealed odd little glares,
'What if I'm brighter than anyone dares?
I might upstage the moon or steal the show!'
The lantern smiled wide, 'Then let's put on a glow!'

Voices Beneath the Eaves

Under the roof, where the chatter won't cease,
A family of squirrels debates over cheese.
'That sharp cheddar's mine!' one screams with a squeak,
While the others roll eyes, 'Oh please, not this week!'

A bird joins the fun with a raucous caw,
'You bunch of nutters, just look at you all!'
Through gaps in the wood, they plot and they scheme,
For dinner tonight, what a glorious dream!

From glistening acorns to berries so sweet,
They argue the best dish, a culinary feat.
With each goofy plan, and yet one too bold,
They end up with crumbs, which they later unload.

As twilight descends, and the party winds down,
They gather around, wearing crumbs like a crown.
With laughter and stories, till they drift into sleep,
Underneath clever roofs, where secrets they'll keep.

Reflections in Glass

In a shop where mirrors play,
I noticed my hair turned gray.
The clerk just grinned, no need to fight,
"Embrace the change, it feels just right!"

I caught a glimpse of a rubber duck,
It floated by, oh what a luck!
"Is that you?" I asked, with a laugh,
He winked and quacked, took a bubble bath.

Outside, the world took a spin,
A cat in a bow tie strutted in.
"Where's the party?" he called with glee,
"Come on, share your secrets with me!"

In every reflection, a giggle spark,
Distorted truths in the day's lark.
Life's a jest, so sing aloud,
Let laughter reign, be joyful and proud!

Shadows of Dreams

In the twilight, shadows crop,
They dance and twirl, they just won't stop.
A shadow cat with a hat too big,
Bopped along, doing a little jig.

A tree waved its branches, oh so proud,
Telling tales to the gathering crowd.
"I once was a seed on a wild, wild spree,
Now look at me! Just a sage, you see!"

The moon cracked jokes about the sun,
"Yo, buddy, ever had a run?
You blaze while I chill and glow at night,
Together we shine—what a delightful sight!"

In our dreams, the shadows prance,
Wit flows like a spontaneous dance.
So let them swirl for all to see,
Life's a stage — just be goofy and free!

The Weaving of Wishes

In a dusty nook, the wishes spun,
A fabric of dreams, oh what fun!
One stitch for laughter, another for glee,
The tapestry grew, as bright as can be.

A wish for ice cream on a summer night,
Popped up, swirling in delight!
"Scoop it high, don't hold back!"
Cried a yarn-ball rolling down the track.

A thread for socks that never lose pairs,
Wove a tale of two silly bears.
"I lost one!" shouted Goldie with flair,
But the other's off dancing, without a care.

Every wish a stitch, every laugh a weave,
Join the fun—so much to believe!
In a world of fabric, bright and bold,
Life's whims are the treasures that we hold!

Shifting Sands of Time

The sands of time, they jiggle and shake,
Tick-tock, tick-tock, and what a break!
A crab in a suit made a toast,
"To moments we treasure, let's party the most!"

A tide of memories, waves on the shore,
Swept in echoes of laughter, always wanting more.
"Time flies fast, just like my hat!"
Chortled a seagull whilst chasing a brat.

Watch the grains, they slide and slip,
Each one a giggle, a trip, a quip.
On this beach, we picnic and dine,
Serving joy with a twist of lime!

So let's not fret, let's just unwind,
In this silly journey, a treasure we find.
With each grain a story, a slight rearrange,
We laugh at the magic that life can exchange!

Haunting at the Intersection

At the corner where shadows play,
A ghostly cat does sway and sway.
It purrs for cars that zoom so fast,
While sipping tea from a teacup vast.

Street signs chatter in a confused tone,
One says 'Left' while another moans.
A bicycle talks to a lamppost bright,
It's a party every day and night.

Mice in suits march to and fro,
Hunting for crumbs that humans throw.
A traffic cone joins in the dance,
Wobbling to a polka trance.

Here laughter echoes, and the jokes flow,
As umbrellas gossip about the snow.
At this jolly junction of fate,
All the mishaps, oh, how they elevate!

A Tapestry of Divergence

Threads of fate begin to weave,
In this place where paths deceive.
A squirrel delivers packages with glee,
While a dog claims it, 'I'm meant to be free!'

Two paths converge with a grin and a jog,
Debating the best route for a lost fog.
The trees gossip about passersby,
While the sun sneaks in with a wink and a sigh.

Cats in sunglasses prance with flair,
Owls recount tales of the local air.
Daffodils debate which way to bloom,
As the mailman rides through nature's room.

And every glance meets a chuckle or two,
At this crossroads where humor flew.
In the tapestry of quirky delight,
Mishaps sparkle under the moonlight.

The Crossways of Memory

At this junction where memories merge,
A bicycle tells tales with a joyful urge.
The clouds bring laughter, raining down cheer,
As lost socks declare, 'We're perfectly here!'

Postcards whisper to the passing breeze,
Reminiscing moments that always please.
Balloons pride their journey, so grand and wide,
While butterflies dance on the funfair ride.

A cat with a monocle peers down the street,
Critiquing the style of the shoes on feet.
Woodpeckers drum to the rhythm of chance,
While neighbors argue about the best dance.

Every corner a giggle, each alley a jest,
In the crossways of memory, humor is best.
So skip down this path of magical play,
Where laughter is mapped out every day!

The Path Less Taken

A signpost winks at the curious soul,
Suggesting detours, not the regular stroll.
A snail races past with great aspiration,
Claiming it's all about the destination!

Raccoons in tuxedos adjust their ties,
Planning a party under the moonlit skies.
Every stone tells a joke, both silly and quaint,
As the path less traveled becomes a complaint.

Pigeons perform their best dance moves,
As a mouse breaks a record, making grooves.
A lollipop tree grows fruits of delight,
Promising sweets to those passing by at night.

With each twist of this whimsical path,
Laughter emerges, defying the math.
So heed the signs leading you astray,
For joy is the prize found in games we play!

Conversations with the Unfamiliar

A cat gave advice, on how to nap,
Wearing a hat, designed for a chap.
A squirrel sold tickets to a nutty show,
While pigeons played cards, all in a row.

A hedgehog in glasses read tales of woe,
As frogs hopped in rhythm, putting on a show.
The tea kettle whistled, inviting them near,
With biscuits that laughed, spreading joy and cheer.

The toaster chimed in, sharing a joke,
While spoons made the moves, like a dance floor provoke.

Chairs joined the laughter, creaking with glee,
As laughter erupted, echoing free.

In this curious place, odd friendships emerge,
With puns and puffs, the quirks they converge.
It's a mad little world, where nothing's too strange,
In conversations of whimsy, all things rearrange.

Paths Yet to Walk

A snail took a poll, on which way to slide,
While ants argued loudly, trying to decide.
The wind picked up pace, showing them tricks,
While butterflies fluttered, plotting new picks.

Each step a surprise, with puddles to skip,
A dance with the breeze, not a thought to grip.
They tripped on their thoughts, flipping like coins,
Unraveled their worries, through laughter they joined.

The grass whispered secrets, as frogs sang along,
With echoes of joy, creating a song.
A pathway called out, with signs made of cheese,
The road less traveled, as sweet as a breeze.

Together they wandered, embracing the new,
With paths yet to walk, under skies vast and blue.
Life's funny like that, a twist or a turn,
Each moment a lesson, for which they all yearn.

Mosaic of Unchosen Journeys

A patchwork of paths, made of mismatched socks,
With buttons for wheels and twine for the locks.
A map drawn in crayon, with scribbles and dots,
Pointing to places where chaos is sought.

Lizards in bowties held grand debates,
On whether to travel or stay with the mates.
Each journey a puzzle, each turn a new game,
With laughter and hiccups that never felt lame.

They filled up their bags with giggles and sighs,
Chasing the sunset and counting the flies.
A compass that spins, never points to a way,
Just leads to adventures, to brighten the day.

In this funny mosaic, both vibrant and wild,
Every misstep crafted, as if by a child.
With each chosen path, they'd cheer and divide,
In a world made of whimsy, where joy is the guide.

Tides of Turmoil

A wave pulled a poodle, straight into a spree,
While crabs played the ukulele, under a tree.
The tide tossed its secrets, in bubbles and foam,
As seagulls debated, what makes a good home.

The ocean flipped over, sharing a grin,
With fish in tuxedos, ready to swim.
They danced on the shore, with shells as their shoes,
Creating a ruckus, each splash was a muse.

A jellyfish juggled, with sparkles and cheer,
While starfish took turns, giving good cheer.
The boat drifted by, its sails full of hope,
With laughter like ripples, they all learned to cope.

In tides of odd turmoil, the chaos was fun,
With waves that would tickle and shine like the sun.
Each splash told a story, of friends in a whirl,
As fun found its place, in this wonderful swirl.

Learning from Liminal Spaces

In the hallway, I trip on a shoe,
Wondering if stepping is what I should do.
Ghosts of decisions float in the air,
Each echoing giggle is hard to compare.

A door swings open, but it's just a cat,
Wearing a hat and looking quite fat.
It blinks at me, unimpressed by my plight,
As I tumble through choices, both wrong and right.

Socks mismatched in this scene of the strange,
Should I dance in delight or spend it to change?
With every step taken, the floorboards squeak,
Guiding me softly, a fate that's unique.

So here in this space, I try to embrace,
The slip and the slide, the joyful misplace.
In laughter, I find the courage to roam,
In this wacky abode, I finally feel home.

Fragments of Uncertainty

Under the stairs, there's a monster of sorts,
Lurking in shadows, wearing strange shorts.
With a wig made of noodles and shoes full of cheese,
It dances and twirls, providing a tease.

The clock on the wall ticks backward in glee,
With hands all askew, what could this all be?
A riddle of time, a puzzle of fate,
Each tick tells a tale of a curious state.

Waffles on Wednesdays, or maybe it's toast?
Who knew breakfast here could be such a boast?
I ponder my options, with giggles I weigh,
The chaos of choices that brighten my day.

So fragments collide, in this fittingly odd,
A medley of moments that leave me awed.
In whispers of wonder, I start to embrace,
The quirks of life's path at each playful space.

Echoing Footsteps

I tiptoe past rooms where the laughter runs wild,
Echoes of footsteps, each door like a child.
A jester appears, juggling socks and some fruit,
As I giggle and dodge—what a strange pursuit!

The hallway's a maze of imaginary friends,
Where the giggles and whispers intertwine and blend.
A trampoline here and a slide over there,
My heart does a flip in the whimsical air.

Each step seems a journey, a dance full of cheer,
With boots left behind by the nobody here.
As I leap from the present to moments unknown,
A symphony of quirks makes me feel at home.

So here's to the echoes, the laughter they bring,
In wobbling footsteps, I find joy in my swing.
With whimsy and wonder, life's giggle parade,
In this inner sanctum, all doubts are delayed.

A Canvas of Possibilities

Colors collide on this whimsical wall,
Each stroke is a giggle, a rise, then a fall.
With paintbrushes dancing in improbable rows,
Each splash and each smear, what mischief it sows!

Dandelions whisper secrets of bright,
In bows and in curls, they invite with delight.
As I frolic through visions of laughter and light,
The absurdity of time pushes me to take flight.

Sprinkles of bright in a cake that won't set,
Plates full of jelly, and I'm having no fret.
With frosting that tickles every taste bud in sight,
Being messy is bliss, oh what a pure bite!

So here on this canvas, I dance and I twirl,
With giggles and colors, my imagination unfurl.
In a swirl of delight, I embrace every brush,
In the realm of possibilities, I'm lost in the hush.

Navigating the In-Between

Two paths diverge in clashing hues,
One's full of chatter, the other, snooze.
I took a step, then slipped and fell,
Into a puddle that rang like a bell.

A squirrel laughed, it chattered away,
'Why choose a route on such a gray day?'
I weighed my options with utmost care,
But pizza was calling—there's joy over there!

Should I dance with a tree or wave at a snail?
Each choice brings a laugh, it never gets stale.
My compass spins wildly, can't find the right path,
But I'll just keep laughing—it's better than math!

In the in-between, where chaos does reign,
I'll take all the wrong turns, ignore all the pain.
With jokes in my pocket and laughter galore,
I'll ride on this whimsy forevermore!

The Junction of Secrets

At the corner where whispers flicker and fade,
A chicken and penguin are planning a parade.
They squawk about ducks who can't quite fly,
While I'm stuck here wondering why I said hi.

Traffic lights wink like they're in on a joke,
A red one yells, 'Hey! Don't be a bloke!'
Green lights a chuckle, yellow makes a pout,
Each tick of the time is another weird route.

A gnome gives directions with grand gestures and flair,
I nod and I smile but don't go anywhere.
A car honks loudly, it's part of the show,
As I dance with my doubts, oh where could we go?

Secrets abound in this quirky old spot,
With laughter and whimsy, I'll give it a shot.
No sense in rushing or feigning a sway,
I'll follow the fun and let life lead the way!

Entrances to Unknown Destinies

One door says 'pizza,' the next greets the sun,
Another door whispers, 'Let's have some fun!'
I thought of the future—too grim to behold,
So I opened the door with the candy, I'm sold!

Inside is a wizard who juggles and sings,
He offers me cupcakes, and oh, what a fling!
A dragon pops in to share some hot tea,
Turns out, they adore my shenanigans, whee!

A staircase is waiting, it wobbles and creaks,
'Take it, dear friend, for adventure it seeks!'
But what if it leads to a wardrobe, I fear,
Where socks just conspire to disappear, oh dear!

Opportunities dance in this whimsical space,
With smiles and surprises that quicken the pace.
I choose the path with a giggle and gleam,
For in this odd entrance, I live out my dream!

Beyond the Veil of Choices

I stood at the curtain, all riddled with doubt,
Behind it lay options—would I scream or shout?
A cat in a top hat winked with a grin,
'Which choice will you make? Let's see who can win!'

I pondered my path, a left or a right,
One path had cake, the other, a fight.
'Twas a close call, but I chose the bake-off,
Where frosting and laughter would never be scoffed.

A llama delivered my flour with style,
As my competitors fainted, unable to smile.
Confetti erupts—it's a sweet-toothed melee,
And my cupcakes, they dance, what a wacky soiree!

Beyond these choices, whimsy does bloom,
Each option a giggle, yet boldly I zoom.
With cake in my heart and joy all around,
In the land of the funny, I've finally found!